The Boy in the Striped Pyjamas

Contents

OXFORD
UNIVERSITY PRESS

Great Clarendon Street, Oxford OX2 6DP

Oxford University Press is a department of the University of Oxford. It furthers the University's objective of excellence in research, scholarship, and education by publishing worldwide in

Oxford New York

Auckland Cape Town Dar es Salaam Hong Kong Karachi Kuala Lumpur Madrid Melbourne Mexico City Nairobi New Delhi Shanghai Taipei Toronto

With offices in

Argentina Austria Brazil Chile Czech Republic France Greece Guatemala Hungary Italy Japan South Korea Poland Portugal Singapore Switzerland Thailand Turkey Ukraine Vietnam

Oxford is a registered trade mark of Oxford University Press in the UK and in certain other countries

Text © John Boyne 2007

British Library Cataloguing in Publication Data

Data available

ISBN: 978-0-19-832683-0

10 9 8

Printed by Printplus, China

Acknowledgements

The Publisher would like to thank the following for permission to reproduce photographs:

P3: John Boyne; p 4t: Ira Nowinski/Corbis; p4bl: Hulton Archive/Getty; p4br: Bettmann/Corbis; p5: Bettmann/Corbis; p14: Oxford University Press.

Illustrations are by Q2A India.

Original cover published by arrangement with Random House Children's Books, one part of the Random House Group Ltd.

We are grateful for permission to reprint the following copyright material in this guide:

John Boyne: extracts from *The Boy in Striped Pyjamas* (David Fickling, 2006), reprinted by permission of the Random House Group Ltd; extracts from interview with Teenreads, interview with The Hindu and notes to the US edition, reprinted by permission of PFD (www.pfd.co.uk) on behalf of the author.

Jim Carrington: review of *The Boy in Striped Pyjamas* from Children's Books UK website, www.cbuk.info, reprinted by permission of Children's Books UK Info and the author.

Anne Holm: extract from *I am David* (Methuen, 1965), copyright © Anne Holm 1963, English translation copyright © Egmont Books Ltd 1965, first published as *David* by Gyldendal, Copenhagen, reprinted by permission of Egmont UK Ltd.

Labi Siffre: 'Something Inside (So Strong)', copyright © 1987 Empire Music Ltd, Universal Music Publishing Ltd, lyrics reprinted by permission of Music Sales Ltd. All rights reserved. International copyright secured.

We have tried to trace and contact all copyright holders before publication. If notified, the publisher will be pleased to rectify any errors or omissions at the earliest opportunity.

Key to icons:

 Pair or group activity

 A resources sheet from the Teacher's Pack supports this activity.

A Letter from John Boyne

In April 2004 an image came into my head of two little boys sitting on either side of a fence, having a conversation, and from that image sprang the novel *The Boy in the Striped Pyjamas*. I knew where the boys were and I knew it was a place where no one should ever have been. I was interested in the journey that would bring them there, their conversations, the things they would have in common, and the necessary end that they would reach.

As I wrote the novel I found that I immediately felt close to my main character, Bruno. I liked his innocence, his charm, his naiveté, his friendliness. I liked the fact that the values he held were better and purer than those of his parents. But I was also faced with many difficult decisions and questions, one of which was the question of how close to the true-life events of the Holocaust I wanted to get. I decided very early on that I did not want to write a novel specifically about Auschwitz or Dachau or any of the camps during that time; I wanted the camp that I created to represent the many death camps which the criminals created around Europe in the early 1940s. This is one of the reasons why the word 'Auschwitz' is never used in the book. And I wanted to broaden out the subject to include those other examples which are perhaps less familiar to younger readers. I wanted to leave young people who read this book questioning the many horrors which have taken place around the world in the 60 years between the liberation of the Second World War camps and today, and asking the simple question: why?

This is a novel which can cause great debate among those who love it and those who hate it, but the great joy of literature (as opposed to politics or religion) is that it embraces differing opinions, it encourages debate, it allows us to have heated conversations with our closest friends and dearest loved ones and through it all no one gets hurt, no one gets taken away from their homes, and no one gets killed.

I do hope you enjoy reading and discussing this book.

John Boyne

John Boyne

'The Final Solution'

'They were everyone' (page 30)

Fact File

The Holocaust happened between 1933 and 1945, when Adolf Hitler, as Chancellor of Germany, used his power and that of his generals to persecute the Jewish people in Germany and beyond. This eventually led to the murder of 6,000,000 Jews and the destruction of 5,000 Jewish communities.

Gradually, the Jewish population of Germany and beyond was separated from the rest of society by special laws, and forced to live in 'ghettos'. These were walled areas away from the rest of the population. Eventually, Jews were rounded up and sent to concentration camps for execution or hard labour.

Arbeit Macht Frei – 'Work will free you'

This is the infamous entrance to Birkenau (Auschwitz II), where Jewish prisoners were sent to be exterminated. The picture is taken from outside the camp. Arbeit Macht Frei was written above the gate, to encourage the Jews who were kept alive to work hard. For most, however, the only 'freedom' they would find would be in death.

One of the four crematoria with gas chambers in Auschwitz II.

This is the place where the newly arrived prisoners were assessed – some (usually about two-thirds) would go straight to the gas chambers. The entire Jewish population from Hungary and Northern Transylvania stopped here.

Final Solution'

...all of them... were wearing the same clothes as each other: a pair of grey striped pyjamas with a grey striped cap on their heads.
(page 38)

Research

Using books and the Internet, see if you can find answers to the following questions:

1   What was 'the final solution'?
2   How many Jews were sent to Auschwitz?
3   What happened to them when they got there?

Who are all those people?... And what are they all doing there?
(page 35)

Research

Later in the story, we learn a little about the Jewish people who lived at Cracow in Poland. Find out the location of Poland and Cracow, and what happened to the Jews who lived there during the time of the Holocaust.

Top search tips!
Try the following websites:
http://en.wikipedia.org/wiki/Auschwitz_concentration_camp
http://isurvived.org
www.holocaustcenter.org
www.iwm.org.uk

Perhaps it's not a farm then... Which means this mightn't be the countryside.
(page 35)

Compare this aerial view of Auschwitz with what you imagined from reading *The Boy in the Striped Pyjamas*. Is it as you thought?

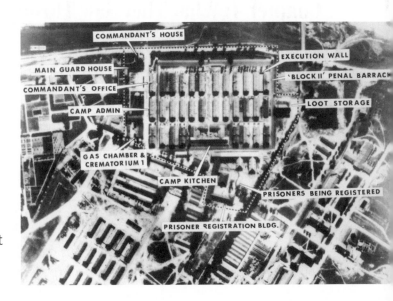

Whose Voice is it Anyway?

Wh

Through the eyes of a child

Some readers feel that the writer has got it wrong about Bruno! They think some of his thoughts and ideas seem too child-like for a boy of nine. They also think that surely Gretel would know more about concentration camps at the age of 12. This is what one reader says:

I thought that Gretel seemed a bit young in her first comments about the camp. Surely she'd know a bit more about her father's job and what was happening to Jewish people!

John Boyne says:

This is perhaps the question I have been asked the most about this novel and I feel very strongly that Bruno's innocence and ignorance are not only crucial to the story, but appropriate to the times, too... When the war ended and the camps were liberated, the world was shocked by what they learned. But it had been going on for years... Purely in terms of my novel, however, I stand by my belief that Bruno is an innocent child in a time and place that he does not understand.

 ## And what do you say?

Look at the following extracts with a partner. Do you think that the children's understanding is too child-like for their ages?

Chapter 4: What They Saw Through the Window

Seeing the children for the first time:

The more they were shouted at, the closer they huddled together, but then one of the soldiers lunged towards them... the soldiers all started to laugh and applaud them. 'It must be some sort of rehearsal,' suggested Gretel...
(page 37)

Chapter 5: Out Of Bounds At All Times and No Exceptions

A boy's salute:

'Heil Hitler,' he said, which, he presumed, was another way of saying, 'Well, goodbye for now, have a pleasant afternoon.' (page 54)

 Prepare a statement to read to the rest of your class, beginning, 'We think that the children's understanding of the camp and the people there is...'

Another child, another time…

Another writer who chooses to show the world through the eyes of a child is Anne Holm. In 1963, she wrote her prize-winning book *I am David*. In it, the main character, a young boy called David, escapes from a concentration camp at the age of 12 after he has been brought up there from a baby. David has known no other world. Gradually, he learns about the world of freedom, but to begin with, he doesn't trust other people at all, as all he has known is cruelty. In the following extract, David sees children playing for the first time. You will see that in many ways, David is just as ignorant of the world as Bruno:

> *He was startled by the sound of voices not far away… It was the sound of children playing and David decided he would watch them. He usually hurried away when he saw children. He was afraid of them. He had never spoken to children and didn't know how to begin… they were much more dangerous than grown-ups… other children would very soon discover that he knew nothing of the things they took for granted. One thing alone would give him away: he had no idea how to play. People were always talking about children playing, but playing seemed to mean so many different things that David had given up trying to find out what it was.*
>
> *I am David by Anne Holm, page 78*

Through the eyes of David

What does David know about childhood?

What does he misunderstand?

What is the effect of his childish viewpoint on you, the reader?

What do you think the writer is trying to say through David's thoughts here?

 Draw some thought bubbles of your own and write in your main ideas about each of these questions.

Fact File

Narrative voice: *The voice of the writer, which could be different from the voice of the person in the story. For example, Anne Holm's voice tells of how terrible life in a concentration camp is for a child. She cleverly uses David's child-like voice to show this view. You'll notice that John Boyne does the same in* The Boy in the Striped Pyjamas.

Prejudice: Barbed Wire in the Mind

Welcome to Auschwitz! Allow me to guide you through…

 With a partner, write down as many words as possible to describe the atmosphere created by the illustration.

How do writers use symbols?

Below are some examples of signs and symbols which have a meaning that most people recognize:

Peace

Love

Death in war, or remembrance

Can you think of how a fence can also be a symbol used by a writer? Share ideas with a partner and then with the rest of the class.

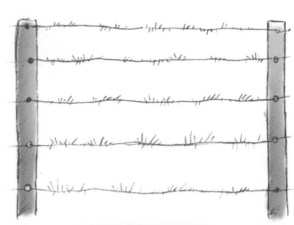

Symbol in The Boy in the Striped Pyjamas

The Boy in the Striped Pyjamas

Barbed Wire in the Mind

'You what?'

Bruno and Shmuel struggle to understand prejudice:

What exactly was the difference? [Bruno] wondered to himself. And who decided which people wore the striped pyjamas and which people wore the uniforms? (page 100)

It was almost (Shmuel thought) as if they were all exactly the same really. (page 204)

Quick Quiz

When Pavel talks to Bruno about his job peeling vegetables and waiting on Bruno's family, he says: Just because a man glances up at the sky at night does not make him an astronomer. (page 82)

Use the following ideas to help you decide what Pavel means.

- ⊙ We cannot always tell what kind of person someone is just from looking at them.
- ⊙ Sometimes people do jobs we would not expect them to do.

Something Inside (So Strong)

by Labi Siffre

The higher you build your barriers
The taller I become
The farther you take my rights away
The faster I will run
You can deny me
You can decide to turn your face away
No matter, cos there's…

Something inside so strong
I know that I can make it
Tho' you're doing me wrong, so wrong
You thought that my pride was gone
Oh no, there's something inside so strong
Oh oh oh oh oh oh something inside so strong

The more you refuse to hear my voice
The louder I will sing
You hide behind walls of Jericho
Your lies will come tumbling
Deny my place in time
You squander wealth that's mine
My light will shine so brightly
It will blind you
Because there's…
Something inside so strong
I know that I can make it

Tho' you're doing me wrong, so wrong
You thought that my pride was wrong
Oh no, there's something inside so strong
Oh oh oh oh oh oh something inside so strong

Brothers and sisters
When they insist we're just not good enough
Well we know better
Just look 'em in the eyes and say
We're gonna do it anyway
We're gonna do it anyway, because there's…

Something inside so strong…

This song was originally written as a protest against apartheid in South Africa – a system which meant that black and white people had to live and work completely separately. All of the wealth and power was with the white population.

Improvise ideas for a speech in which Pavel speaks his thoughts to Lieutenant Kotler. Try to capture the same tone as the song by Labi Siffre. Record three or four sentences that could be included in a poem.

Friendship: A Way Under the Fence

'We're like twins'

When Bruno and Shmuel first meet they realize that not only are they the same age, but they were actually born on the same day! Gradually, as the story unfolds, their friendship deepens. However, like in all friendships, they must learn to trust and care for each other. In Chapter 15, Bruno pretends that he does not know Shmuel, as he is so afraid of Lieutenant Kotler. Bruno is then terrified that Shmuel will no longer be his friend.

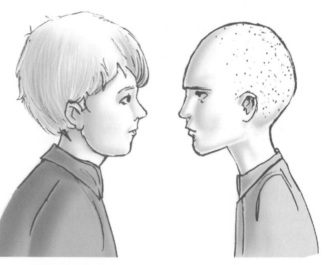

Sculpting the scene

Exploring through drama

Using the following extract as a basis for your sculpture, sculpt the characters into the exact bodily positions you think they should be in at this moment in the story. Then, to capture the full dramatic effect, the sculptor can read the extract out loud:

'Your...?' began Lieutenant Kotler, looking across at Bruno in confusion. He hesitated. 'What do you mean he's your friend?' he asked. 'Do you know this boy, Bruno?'

Bruno's mouth dropped open and he tried to remember the way you used your mouth if you wanted to say the word 'yes'. He'd never seen anyone look so terrified as Shmuel did at that moment and he wanted to say the right thing to make things better, but then he realized that he couldn't; because he was feeling just as terrified himself...

'I've never spoken to him,' said Bruno immediately. 'I've never seen him before in my life. I don't know him.'

(pages 171–172)

'I like sitting here and talking'

Shmuel's viewpoint is really only seen through what he says. Only occasionally does John Boyne tell us what he is thinking, because he has chosen to present the story from Bruno's point of view. In fact, we are sometimes left wondering what Shmuel thinks of their friendship!

Spotlight on Shmuel

Here are some questions we asked Shmuel in an imaginary interview. We need your help to decide the answers that Shmuel would be most likely to give. Watch out, though: you'll have to find evidence to back up your choices!

Interviewer: How did you feel when you first met Bruno?
Shmuel: To be honest, I felt…
- happy
- curious
- confused.

Interviewer: How did you feel when he suggested you should come to his house for dinner?
Shmuel: Well, at the time I was…
- pleased
- afraid
- not convinced it was a good idea.

Interviewer: What did you feel when he asked you not to hate his father?
Shmuel: Thinking back, I was…
- angry with him for not understanding the evil of the soldiers
- glad that Bruno was loyal to his father
- ashamed that I should hate my best friend's father
- confused that the two could even be related!

They have to be kept... with the other Jews, Bruno. Didn't you know that?... They can't mix with us. (page 182)

Have you seen him before? Have you talked to him? Why does he say you're his friend? (page 172)

What do you mean there are hundreds of children over there?... What do you know of what goes on over there? (page 191)

Violence and Evil

The problem of violence: a writer's dilemma

The violence of the Holocaust is a difficult subject, even in an adult book, so John Boyne had to be careful not to horrify his young readers. Yet he has said that he does not believe there is any subject that is inappropriate to discuss with children:

It comes down to how we – as parents, teachers or society – decide to introduce them to these matters without trivialising them or patronising our audience. As a writer, one must approach the subject with respect and sensitivity but there's also a responsibility to tell an emotionally honest story that should, ideally, resonate with children and adults alike…

 With a partner, find the following quotation on pages 148–149 of the book: …*none of them could watch.* How is this hint at violence more powerful than if John Boyne had described in graphic detail what happened next?

Exploring through film

'…it made Bruno cry and Gretel grow pale'

The following extract shows Kotler's treatment of Pavel, when he spills the bottle of wine in his lap at dinner:

What happened then was both unexpected and extremely unpleasant. Lieutenant Kotler grew very angry with Pavel and no one – not Bruno, not Gretel, not Mother and not even Father – stepped in to stop him doing what he did next, even though none of them could watch. Even though it made Bruno cry and Gretel grow pale. (pages 148–149)

Storyboarding the scene

Continue the two-frame storyboard below, which shows the incident where Kotler is violent towards Pavel. Try to devise the next three frames.

Violence and Evil

Under the fence and into the darkness

Structural patterning emphasizes that the cruelty is everywhere

Emphasizes theme of prejudice and division

Contrast used very effectively: laughter of soldiers and 'staring' of prisoners

Layered adjectives (noun phrases)

Close-up on camp life

A student has text-marked this extract, to show how the writer creates a vivid picture:

In one corner Bruno could see _three_ soldiers who seemed to be in charge of a group of about _twenty men_. They were shouting at them, and some of the men had fallen to their knees and were remaining there _with their heads in their hands_.

In another corner he could see more soldiers standing around and laughing and _looking down the barrels of their guns, aiming them in random directions_, but not firing them.

In fact everywhere he looked, all he could see was _two different types of people_: either _happy, laughing, shouting_ soldiers in their uniforms or _unhappy, crying_ people in _their striped pyjamas_, most of whom seemed to be staring into space _as if they were actually asleep_. (page 208)

Contrast in numbers: sense of unfairness

Reader is invited to speculate why: fear, despair, sorrow?

Creates feeling of menace and potential for deadly violence

Suggests that prisoners are child-like and adds to sense of their vulnerability

Simile suggests the numbness of the sufferers

Reading into writing

Below is an example of taking ideas from the annotated text to make a Point, Evidence, Explanation text in response to the question: 'How does the writer use language effectively to present the violence in this extract?'

Point: In this extract, the writer contrasts the soldiers with the prisoners by using powerful noun phrases.

Evidence: '… either happy, laughing, shouting soldiers in their uniforms or unhappy, crying people in their striped pyjamas…'

Explanation: What makes this effective is not only the contrasting adjectives, but also the different status of the people according to their 'uniforms' or 'pyjamas'.

Now have a go at drafting your own PEE statement, answering the same question.

Causing a Stir!

Whatever you think about *The Boy in the Striped Pyjamas*, it definitely causes a big stir with readers – often leading them to very different views! Some feel that the novel treats the horror of the Holocaust too lightly, while others feel that a child's-eye viewpoint helps to emphasize the horror even more. Here are some readers' reactions:

Have a debate: hammer it out!

Up for debate: Does *The Boy in the Striped Pyjamas* deal with the sensitive subject of the Holocaust in an appropriate way?

These should get your ideas flowing…

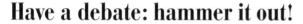

'It's a really good book if you are 11 or older, but younger audiences might not understand the plot of this masterpiece!' Nahdia, 11, Ealing

'I loved it, mainly because of all the brilliant characters. I got addicted, and at the end, I even cried!' Carmel, 15, Tewkesbury

'A powerful and chilling book. It jolts readers with a horrible shock in the final pages.' Manjit, 12, Dover

'Bruno is too naive for his age.' Paul, 14, Cardiff

'The style is too simple. I'm not sure it works.' Charmaine, 15, Uxbridge

I think that when Bruno says, 'Was it your bicycle?' on page 175, it's really insensitive to what children like Shmuel went through in the Holocaust.

I think that the effect of Bruno's death on his father on page 215 is an amazing way of showing the horror of the Holocaust.

The final line of Chapter 19 shows just how seriously John Boyne treats this issue and how much he wants his reader to be affected.

I think that what happens to Pavel, who was a kind doctor who used his life to help people, really shows how stupid and cruel the Holocaust was.

Causing a Stir!

Surfing for a review

Strong adjective

Title of book included in first sentence

Quite an informal style

Review by Jim Carrington

The Boy in the Striped Pyjamas is an extraordinary book in many ways. For a start, it has no blurb – or at least not an ordinary blurb – but instead some text on the flyleaf simply encourages the reader to read the book without prior knowledge of what it is about.

Written in the present tense: the book is being read now

Written in the first person so that the view given seems personal

Although that might seem like a particularly see-through sales pitch, I would have to agree with the staff at David Fickling; I shared the ignorance of the main character Bruno, which made the reality of Auschwitz and the sudden realisation that the pyjamas referred to in the title were those belonging to Jews, as they waited to be gassed, all the more shocking.

Gives name of main character

Tells the reader where and when the book is set

This is the story of Bruno, a young boy, moved from Berlin to somewhere he calls Outwith. Through Bruno's often unbelievably naive experiences, the reader gets to witness the inhumanity of the Nazi party and the sickening stupidity of Auschwitz. Despite his surroundings, Bruno lives without prejudice and soon forms a friendship with Shmuel: the boy in the striped pyjamas. Their friendship – one that should be an example to the adults around them – is conducted in secret and through the fence. This friendship is ended in the most tragic way.

Brief outline of story

A few relevant details about the story

Noun phrases paint a powerful picture

John Boyne's novel is perhaps most remarkable for the restraint which he shows in telling his story: the mood throughout is calm and free from prejudice. This allows the events of the story to unfold in all their inhumanity and shows many of the adults in the story to be weak and scared people, carrying out actions which they ordinarily would abhor.

Gives away the tragic end but not the details

Reasons why he likes the book

This is a book which demands to be read in schools, as a cautionary tale about hatred, as a vital look at the lives of German and Jewish children in the war, and as an example of how to write stories that gain all their power by not trying too hard.

More strong adjectives

Final paragraph sums up the impact of the book

Jim Carrington is a primary school teacher in London.

A brief note on the author of the review

Hints at the personalities of the characters

Suggests who would like the book

Special assignment

The Reading Connects website has asked you to provide a review of The Boy in the Striped Pyjamas. You should use the following structure:

- ◉ About the author
- ◉ About the story (not the end!)
- ◉ What's good about the book?
- ◉ Any weak points?
- ◉ Would you recommend it to a friend? If so, to whom?

Pathways... to Another Good Read

Here are some ideas which could help you to explore the novel further. You could:

- ◉ carry out some further research into the novel as a fable – John Boyne talks about this on his website, www.johnboyne.com
- ◉ continue your study of the morality tale (a popular genre in fiction)
- ◉ do some further empathy work on Father, Mother and Gretel following the end of the story
- ◉ have a class discussion on the likely fate of Kotler and Pavel
- ◉ carry out some research into songs that are used for political protest
- ◉ write a letter to the author about the more controversial aspects of the novel such as, the viewpoint
- ◉ produce a screenplay for a film of the novel.

Thematically-linked books

Children and war

I am David by Anne Holm
ISBN 0-74-970136-6
This is the moving story of a boy who escapes from a concentration camp. Gradually, he awakens to knowledge of the outside world.

The Endless Steppe by Esther Hautzig
ISBN 978-006-447027-8
This is the incredible but true story of how a family of Jewish Poles are sent to Siberia during the Second World War. The narrative follows their brave struggle to cope.

The Silver Sword by Ian Serraillier
ISBN 0-14-030146-1
The Balicki family are torn apart by the Germans and taken from their home in Warsaw, Poland, in 1940. Centring on the children of the family, the book follows their journey to Switzerland, as they try to reunite with their parents.

Friedrich by Edite Kroll and Hans Peter Richter
ISBN 0-14-032205-1
While growing up together, two boys, a German and a Jew, become friends. The story goes on to follow the brutal hardships of the young Jewish boy and his family during the Holocaust.

Goodnight Mister Tom by Michelle Magorian
ISBN 0-14-130144-9
This is the wonderful story of a displaced and abused boy who escapes his violent background and also the London Blitz, to find a new life in the country with Mr Tom.

Racial prejudice

The Skin I'm In by Sharon G. Flake
ISBN 978-019-832675-5
This is the story of a clever and unique young black girl, and her struggle to make sense of both her own hopes and fears and the complex society in which she lives.

Non-fiction

I Have Lived a Thousand Years: Growing Up in the Holocaust by Livia Bitton-Jackson
ISBN 0-74-340875-6
The true story of a young Jewish Hungarian girl, whose family is gradually deprived of liberty and eventually forced to live in a ghetto. There is only one way out of the ghetto: into a labour camp.

The Diary of Anne Frank by Anne Frank
ISBN 014-131518-0
The famous story of a young Jewish girl and her family who are forced into hiding by the Nazis during the Second World War.

The Boy in the Striped Pyjamas